DEDICATED TO:

ALL HARD–WORKING AMERICAN TAXPAYERS.

WE SALUTE AND HONOR YOU.

TAKE COURAGE. YOU WILL SOON BE FREE.

ABOUT THE AUTHORS

Paul S. Damazo

Mr. Damazo is a registered Industrial Engineer, businessman and consultant for the past thirty years in America and overseas. He has taught 12 years as an associate professor at Loma Linda University, 4 years part time professor at UCLA, and 4 years part time at La Sierra University.

Paul started his first business at age eleven. Since then, he started, grew and sold ten other businesses. He last employed 2500. He started with one employee, and the business grew to ninety in the first six months and 2500 within five years.

Mr. Damazo is the founder/director/speaker for the famous Wealth Creation and Wealth Preservation seminars, which he has given for the past fifteen years nation wide.

Mr. Damazo is a philanthropist and author of four books. His last book was a masterpiece entitled "20 Proven Ways to Become a Millionaire," which received two national awards.

He has been on television and radio from Hawaii to Maine for the past three years. As a result of his selfless dedication to others, he has helped hundreds of thousands have a better life.

Leo Schreven,

International life mastery coach and motivational speaker Leo Schreven, "The Energizer Bunny," is known world wide as the "Machine gun speaker" because holds audiences spellbound by his energy, humor and rapid-fire delivery. He has lived more in 50 years than most people do in ten lifetimes. He is a businessman, entrepreneur, author, motivational speaker, TV personality, and the husband of one wife who deserves a medal for putting up with him for 28 years of marriage. He is an extreme sportsman who loves fishing, hunting, skydiving, skiing, scuba, and anything dangerous enough to cause his mother to pray without ceasing. He has one daughter and lives in a log cabin in the mountains of North East Washington with Canada right out his back door. He has traveled and spoken in nearly every country of the world, and has more air miles than most angels. A cowboy at heart, he loves horses and ranching. The son of a poor immigrant family, he has risen to become a wonderful success story and inspiration to others.

Leo devotes over 300 days a year to travel and to speak to audiences, encouraging them to grow and reach heights they never thought possible. His non-profit ministry provides free seminars and materials worldwide and ⅓ of his year is spent in volunteer labor worldwide. His signature "All Power Seminar" is a series of 20 seminars that teach people to master their physical, mental, emotional, spiritual, and financial lives.

He is not politically correct and proud of it. Leo shoots straight; you never have to second-guess what he thinks or says, which makes some folks squirm in their britches, but he always does it with love and genuine care. His motto is: "What's the use of living if you don't feel alive? His pet peeve is: "Out of touch politicians." His favorite saying is: "At the end it is not how many breaths you took that matter. It is how many moments you spent that took your breath away."

On May 19, 2011, Leo turned 50. To celebrate, he walked across America in 100 days, one of only four people to do so. With the same tenacity and will power to overcome impossible odds, Leo is ready to take on American taxpayers' biggest problem, the IRS.

He may even run for president someday....

CLOSE THE IRS, NOW
(THE NUTSHELL VERSION)

1. We are leading a movement to do away with the IRS and the current personal and corporate tax system.

2. We are providing a solution called, "The National 10% Sales Tax." It is a simple alternative to the complex current tax system. A 10% sales tax is added to anything anyone buys in America except education and medical items. That's it. It is so simple it can be explained in 4 words: YOU BUY, YOU PAY. The 10% National Sales Tax will bring in more revenue than what the IRS is currently collecting.

3. For you it means no more IRS forms, no deductions, no paperwork, no April 15, no audits, no corporate or personal income tax. The IRS will be gone, and you'll never have to deal with anything any more as far as tax.

4. For Americans it means everyone is equal, and everyone legal or illegal is treated the same. We all pay the same percentage.

5. It will gradually help reduce our national debt, bring millions of jobs back to America, and cause a massive stimulus to our economy.

5. Forget the flat tax or VAT tax, etc. Most alternatives are simply additions to our current tax system and will make it only more complicated. We do not want to add to the complexity; we are doing away with the IRS and current tax system completely.

6. There are 545 politicians, senators, congressmen, Supreme Court justices, and the president, who are responsible for the current tax system and the $15 trillion dollars (and still counting) of debt they have caused Americans. There are 313 million Americans like you. We outnumber them 610,000 to 1. We pay their salaries. We tell them what to do.

7. You need to take action today to vote and make your voice heard.

    A. Go online to <u>www.closetheirstoday.com</u> and vote. We need millions of votes to force Congress to abolish the IRS and adopt to a 10% National Sales Tax.

    B. We are asking every American to make an annual $10.00 investment to help raise the needed funds to push this through Congress.

Roll up your sleeves and have fun, because we're taking down the IRS.

TABLE OF CONTENTS

INTRODUCTION

One thing unites Americans: We all hate the IRS.

This book is a call to action.

WE, THE AMERICAN PEOPLE, ARE GOING
TO ABOLISH THE IRS!

We've had it.

This blood sucking government leech is the most illegal, feared, time consuming, wealth wasting and corrupt institution in America. Seven million words now fill a tax code that even the incompetent government leaders, who voted it through, can't figure out.

Americans don't want to fill out tax forms; our time is too valuable. We don't want to spend hours trying to figure out what we can or can't deduct. We're sick of getting letters from the IRS that waste our time. And we're really fed up with the fear tactics and oppression of the government.

IT'S OVER.

The power is with you, the people. We will overthrow this. This book is a simple step-by-step plan to do it. This book is about a far better alternative. In the pages ahead you will see how you can accomplish this.

- Pass it on. Together we can rally millions of Americans.
- Vote your support at the website: www.closetheirsnow.com
- Join the organized rallies across the country.
- Become a member of HEIRS.

Help
Eliminate
I
R
S

HEIRS is a new Division of the All Power Seminar Corporation, and it is leading this revolution to close the IRS.

I'm Leo Schreven and I'm leading this movement with Paul Damazo. We are both businessmen. Paul is now in Loma Linda California after building a dozen successful business corporations. He is also the author of the famous book, "80 Proven Ways To Become A Millionaire." He has donated many millions of dollars to charity over his lifetime.

I'm a motivational speaker, business owner, and run a Life Mastery educational center called All Power Seminars. I recently walked across America in 100 days, talking to thousands of great American people like you. You can watch the whole event at my website: www.allpowerseminar.com.

Every time the American people have rallied together for a common cause, we have won. This time will be no different.

Read this book, and purchase one for every one of your friends and family to read. Pass it on. We want to go viral as fast as we can through social media. Vote online at: www.closetheirsnow.com Get involved. And remember, IT'S YOUR MONEY, NOT THE GOVERNMENT'S! Success is not a question; it is just a matter of time. Come join the rally.

Leo Schreven
Paul Damazo

PS. If you want a quick review of 100 of the most common taxes you pay on top of your personal income tax, enjoy the next few pages. Have a bottle of Pepto-Bismol nearby, though.

1. Personal/Consumer Taxes & Fees
2. Federal income tax
3. State income tax
4. Local income tax
5. Employee social security tax (your employer pays the other half)
6. Employee Medicare tax (your employer pays the other half)
7. Property taxes
8. Road toll charges
9. State sales tax
10. Driver's license renewal fee
11. TV Cable/Satellite fees & taxes
12. Federal telephone surtax, excise tax, and universal surcharge
13. State telephone excise tax and surcharge
14. Telephone minimum usage and recurring/nonrecurring charges tax
15. Gas/electric bill fees & taxes
16. Water/sewer fees & taxes
17. Cigarette tax
18. Alcohol tax
19. Federal gasoline tax
20. State gasoline tax
21. Local gasoline tax
22. Federal inheritance tax
23. State inheritance tax
24. Gift tax
25. Bridge toll charges

26. Marriage license
27. Hunting license
28. Fishing license
29. Bike license fee
30. Dog permit/license
31. State park permit
32. Watercraft registration & licensing fees
33. Sports stadium tax
34. Bike/nature trail permit
35. Court case filing fee
36. Retirement account early withdrawal penalty
37. Individual health insurance mandate tax
38. Hotel stay tax
39. Plastic surgery surcharge
40. Soda/fatty-food tax
41. Air transportation tax
42. Electronic transmission of tax return fees
43. Passport application/renewal fee
44. Luxury & gas-guzzler car taxes
45. New car surcharge
46. License plate and car ownership transfer taxes
47. Yacht and luxury boat taxes
48. Jewelry taxes & surcharges
49. State/local school tax
50. Recreational vehicle tax
51. Special assessments for road repairs or construction
52. Gun ownership permit
53. Kiddie tax (IRS form 8615)
54. Fuel gross receipts tax
55. Waste Management tax
56. Oil and gas assessment tax
57. Use taxes (on out-of-state purchase)

58. IRA rollover tax/withdrawal penalties
59. Tax on non-qualified health saving account distributions
60. Individual and small business surtax (page 336 of Obamacare)
61. Estimated income tax underpayment penalty
62. Alternative Minimum Tax on income Business Taxes & Fees
63. Federal corporate income tax
64. State corporate income tax
65. Tax registration fee for new businesses
66. Employer social security tax
67. Employer Medicare tax
68. Federal unemployment tax
69. State unemployment tax
70. Business registration renewal tax
71. Worker's compensation tax
72. Tax on imported/exported goods
73. Oil storage/inspection fees
74. Employer health insurance mandate tax
75. Excise Tax on Charitable Hospitals (page 2001/Sec. 9007 of Obamacare)
76. Tax on Innovator Drug Companies (Page 2010/Sec. 9008 of Obamacare)
77. Tax on Medical Device Manufacturers (Page 2020/Sec. 9009 of Obamacare)
78. Tax on Health Insurers (Page 2026/Sec. 9010 of Obamacare)
79. Excise Tax on Comprehensive Health Insurance Plans, i.e. "Cadillac" plans
80. Tax on indoor tanning services
81. Utility users tax
82. Internet transaction fee (passed in California; being considered in other states and at federal

level)

83. Professional license fee (accountants, lawyers, barbers, dentists, plumbers, etc.)
84. Franchise business tax
85. Tourism and concession license fee
86. Wiring inspection fees
87. Household employment tax
88. Biodiesel fuel tax
89. FDIC tax (insurance premium on bank deposits)
90. Electronic waste recycling fee
91. Hazardous material disposal fee
92. Food & beverage license fee
93. Estimated income tax underpayment penalty
94. Building/construction permit
95. Zoning permit
96. Fire inspection fee
97. Well permit tax
98. Sales and Use tax seller's permit
99. Commercial driver's license fee
100. Bank ATM transaction tax
101. Occupation taxes and fees (annual charges required for a host of professions)

CHAPTER 1
What American Taxpayers Hate

As an honest American, do you find yourself working longer hours, doing the work of three people for a dollar that reaches half as far as it used to?

Are you increasingly angry that you have to work five months of the year and give it all to a system that places your future, the future of your children, and the future of our nation on the precipice?

Would you like to see a change that allows you to keep most of that money, a super-simple system that levels the playing field for *all* Americans, a system that ends your nightmare of trying to figure out your tax documents so you never have to file again, a system that places the American Dream back within your reach and pays down the national debt instead of increasing it?

Yes?

Me too.

I want you to know that you have far more power to change this situation than you imagine. I also want you to know that if you do not exercise your power, others who do not care about the future of your business, your job, or your children will be more than happy to exercise it for you.

My name is Leo Schreven. I am a husband and father, a loyal American, and a successful businessman. I know that you are as busy as I am, so I will be respectful of your time. If nothing else, please go to the website www.closetheirsnow.com and cast your vote. It is worth hundreds of thousands of dollars to you and your children.

Let's begin.

COUNTLESS CRIMINALS, CHEATERS, CROOKS, THIEVES, ROBBERS AND LIARS HAVE BEEN MADE BY CONGRESS AND PRESIDENTS OVER THE LAST FEW DECADES. HOW? THROUGH THE IRS—THE SINGLE WORST GOVERNMENT INSTITUTION IN U. S. HISTORY.

Why are we maintaining a worthless, diabolical, broken tax system that is tearing the country apart and is not sustainable?

Honest taxpayers by the tens of millions are fed up and ready to explode. Honest taxpayers are actually paying 238% more in taxes because:

*Forty-four million of all U.S. adults do not pay one penny in income tax per year.

*Millions more who are making anywhere from $50,000 per year to millions per year do not even file a return.

*There are tens of millions more that cheat on their taxes year after year using every conceivable way they can contrive. It would take several books just to list and explain the multiple tax evasion systems being used today.

HONEST TAX PAYERS ARE SICK AND TIRED OF MANY OF OUR CORRUPT POLITICIANS WHO THINK OUR HARD EARNED MONEY IS THEIR SLUSH FUND TO SPEND AS THEY SEE FIT.

It is time for the president and Congress to shut

down the IRS and come up with a simple substitute. That is the purpose of this book. And yes, the solution is brilliantly simple (See chapter 4).

I am not against IRS agents and the IRS employees. They are hard working Americans, as you and I are. Let's put the heat where it belongs.

Memorize this. There are:

One hundred senators,

435 congressmen,

1 president,

9 Supreme Court justices.

This equates to 545 human beings who are *responsible* for this atrocity we call the IRS. If these people worked for you and me, they would be fired overnight for incompetence and criminal activity. These 545 people alone pass income tax laws that are signed by the President then sent to the U.S. Treasury, which is responsible for the IRS. In turn, the IRS agents have the unappreciated job of collecting the income taxes based on the tax code Congress passes.

But guess what? There are 313 million Americans. We outnumber them 610,000 to 1. My fellow Americans—rise up! We have the power. We can force them to do what we want. We pay their salaries. Lets take back the power!

THE CURRENT TAX SYSTEM IS ARCHAIC
AND NO ONE IN AMERICA UNDERSTANDS
IT, INCLUDING THE CURRENT AND PAST
IRS TAX COMMISSIONERS.

Some time ago a highly respected financial company (who requested not to be named) had their top tax professionals prepare the data for a typical family tax return, and then sent it to forty-five professional tax preparers in forty-five different cities across a large number of states. *Would you believe not one tax preparation company came up with the correct amount of tax due!* The shocker was that all forty-five professionals were wrong. The range in numbers was from 123% too much tax paid to 14% tax owed.

OTHER THINGS HONEST TAX PAYERS HATE

1. Form 1040 used to be two pages. Today it is 126 pages. Does any American, like me, think that is just plain stupid and complicated?

2. The IRS prints 1,101 different forms. *They* don't even know what form to use. You and I should vote that we use all these forms for toilet paper in the White House and Capitol building for the next 200 years.

3. There are 16,000 pages of instructions for us to use when preparing our income tax. At that rate, the American people have to read only 44 pages a day all year to figure it out.

4. One thousand bills were filed by the 111th Congress just to correct or amend the IRS code. Then, 4,428 additional changes or corrections to the IRS code were voted in the past ten years. Are you feeling crazy yet?

5. Some time ago the IRS was eight years behind because of presidents signing so many new tax laws.

6. Honest taxpayers hate pork barrel tax laws that enable dishonest politicians to get re-elected at the taxpayer expense. Crooked

politicians that do this should be fired on the spot, put in jail for fifteen years, and have all pensions and benefits for him and his family canceled. But, wait—if we did that, we would have no one left in Congress to use all the new IRS toilet paper.

7. Many "give away" government programs are loaded with outright stealing. We have way too many "give away programs" and insufficient investigators. There should never be another socialist program until we have locked the barn doors on all existing fraud in the programs that we have already. Imagine how much our taxes would drop by just enforcing this one area.

8. It is beyond comprehension how our federal government, as well as the governor of Texas and the governor of California, have signed into law "university paid tuition for illegal aliens." But this is just the beginning. Already California politicians are being pushed to include room and board and only God knows what is next. These same politicians give all kinds of our tax money and services to the illegal aliens.

Hey, Washington, please open your dictionary, and look up the term, "illegal aliens." I thought you took a vow to uphold the laws and constitution? *These illegal aliens broke U.S. laws when they entered our country illegally. This makes them law breakers or criminals,* and yet we legal Americans have to work longer and harder to pay for these criminals. Are you as mad about this as I am?

Get ready for more illegals from around the world

coming to the U.S.A. in order to take advantage of all of our free "give away" programs while we taxpayers work harder to pay these unjustified obligations.

9. The present tax system is ruining the quality of life for the honest taxpayer.
10. The president and all Congressmen know there is NO HOPE for the present tax system. They should work diligently to change to a simple national sales tax as outlined in this book. The government is fighting a losing battle on the current income tax system. It will never change. To do this subject justice would take volumes of books. This is just the tip of the iceberg of what the taxpayers hate about the current broken down, worthless tax system.

THE TAXPAYER

"That is someone who works for the federal government but does not have to take the civil service examination."

Ronald Reagan

ONE MORE GROUP YOU REALLY NEED TO HATE

Before closing this chapter you need to know about the second most corrupt group of people in Washington D.C., after the 545 politicians. The lobbyists. There are tens of thousands of lobbyist in D.C. alone.

The definition of a lobbyist, according to Webster, is "a person acting for a special interest group, who tries to influence the voting on legislation or the decisions of government administrators."

This has been going on for many decades, and the hard working taxpayers who know about it are furious. We want all taxpayers to know about it so we can put a final end to this corrupt, criminal practice, which goes on daily and is costing the American taxpayers huge sums.

Corrupt, criminal lobbyists soon buy out the majority of legislators who go to Washington with good intentions. Fellow Americans, it is time to get angry and shut them all down. We are more than able to do so together.

If our founding fathers came up from the grave today and saw how corrupt Washington is, they would give lobbyist twenty-four hours to leave town or go to jail. They would immediately fire all the 545 corrupt politicians and put them all in jail as well.

American citizens vote for our senators and congressman, expecting them to go to Washington, stay honest, clean, and stay free from the criminal and corrupt activities. They are to pass laws to protect America and not special interest groups.

You would be shocked at how many laws are written by lobbyists rather than by our congressmen, all for special interest groups, or for various corporations, all at the taxpayers' expense.

Lobbyist uses numerous types of gifts as bribes to win over Congress to participate in illegal and corrupt criminal activity, and we the taxpayers are footing the bill.

It is time to act. It is our country, our money. We the people demand the change. Abolish the IRS now, and use instead the simple solution in chapter 4.

CHAPTER 2
History of the IRS, and The One Law That Duped All Taxpayers

As a proud citizen of the USA, do you find yourself losing faith in a government that is irresponsible and that does not even listen to you?

Are you completely frustrated at the hassle of doing your taxes every year?

Can you imagine how happy you would be if you never had to worry about April 15 again, never had to file another return, and never had to think about another deduction?

They say the only thing we learn from history is that we don't learn from history. So let's get a short history lesson.

The Boston Tea Party of December 16, 1773, is a major misnomer. It was not a party. It was a planned insurrection against the established authority, Great Britain, which claimed to have control over colonies. The cause of the rebellion was over taxes imposed on the imports from Great Britain to the colonies without consent.

On December 16, 1773, the English East India Co. had several cargo ships full of tea in the Boston harbor. Americans resisted the collection of the tax. A conference was held in the Old South meeting House in Boston, after which sixty men disguised as Indians boarded the vessels and threw 342 chests of tea into the water. Unjust taxes charged by a distant federal government, Britain, was one of the main causes of the colonies war for independence. So began America's hate for taxation, and it continues today. Americans are at the revolt stage again.

EVERY AMERICAN TODAY NEEDS TO SEE
THEMSELVES AS ONE OF THOSE INDIANS.

From the beginning, our young nation preferred to raise needed, limited funds from customs and tariffs; that, basically, means they taxed goods and services that were sold to the public, and not personal income. When Alexander Hamilton became the first Secretary of the Treasury, he prevailed upon our small Congress to set up a system of excise taxes. That was the beginning of property tax, alcohol, sugar, snuff and bond taxes.

When Thomas Jefferson became president he ran on an anti-government platform. He got Congress to repeal all taxes. The government got along well on revenues from tariffs until the War of 1812. To support the War of 1812, Congress levied a direct tax with a quota on each of the eighteen states, plus the first sales tax in U.S. history on luxury items.

Congress again did away with this income tax in 1817. This was the second time in twenty years. For the next forty-five years the federal government paid for itself through tariffs. America *prospered* as a result.

Today's IRS goes back to the Civil War, when, on July 1, 1862, President Lincoln signed into law what was then the most sweeping revenue-producing measure in the nation's history, thus creating the office of Commissioner of Internal Revenue, which set the stage for our modern system of taxation. That was 150 years ago. Twenty million dollars was collected in the first year of operation, with a staff of 4,400 employees just four years later.

However, Congress voted once again to eliminate income tax in 1872. From 1868 to 1913, ninety per-cent of all taxes collected came from distilled spirits, tobacco and fermented liquors.

Then, in 1895, the Supreme Court struck down the income tax as unconstitutional. Please, I wish we had a Supreme Court with those kinds of principles today. Unfortunately in 1909, President William Taft worked out a compromise with Congress, amending the Constitution and giving the government power to collect income tax. Also in 1909, Congress passed the first tax on corporations.

In 1913, Congress passed another amendment to the Constitution, which three-fourths of the states rat-ified and the 16th Amendment was created. This per-mitted the federal government to tax the income of individuals from whatever source derived.

Then the War Revenue Act of 1917, passed by Con-gress, gave immense measure to increase all types of taxes. A total of $153 billion of taxes were collected during World War II, leaving a debt of $280 billion at the end of the war.

THE TAX LAW THAT DUPED ALL TAX-PAYERS

Every time you look at your payroll check and stub, think about Beardsley Rumi. After Pearl Harbor, Congress passed radical increases in income tax. For the first time tens of millions of Americans who never paid taxes before were now having to pay.

The problem was that Americans were not prepared for the annual tax bill now due March 15. In fact, only five percent of the thirty-five million were saving for the annual tax. The federal government, U.S. Treasury and the IRS were all petrified. They did all sorts of things to get taxpayers to start saving for their annual income tax payment, but to no avail. As March 15 approached, Secretary of the Treasury Henry Margenthan, Jr., confronted his colleagues in the treasury, Federal Reserve and the IRS about the nightmarish possibility of very little tax being collected on March 15. In this meeting, Beardsley Rumi, chairman of the Federal Reserve Bank of New York, came up with a plan that duped taxpayers then, and every taxpayer since then.

Four concepts were developed thanks to Rumi. They were:

1. Put wages and salaries on a withholding basis.
2. Start at the beginning of the year rather than the end.
3. A "pay as you go" system.
4. Withhold taxes at the source.

Congress passed it with glee and the president signed it, the most important tax law in decades. The result was the creation of the modern era of tax collection through enactment of the Tax Payment Act of 1945, which has been the president and congressmen's delight over the decades. Why?

1. They can increase our taxes at will.
2. They get their money out of us before we ever see our income.
3. The states can join the bandwagon to get all the money they want in the same way.
4. Our presidents and congressmen over the years have used our hard earned money as

their perpetual slush fund to use as they see fit, with no regard for our hard work to earn our wages.

This withholding system has totally confused the hard working American taxpayers.

If you want to have some fun, go ask 100 people at random how much total tax they pay. I guarantee only one or two can give you even a ballpark figure. Why? Your Federal and State income tax is withheld each paycheck. At the end of the year you have to pay the balance due by April 15, or you also might get a refund.

This, my fellow American, is the reason our government spends trillion of dollars in unnecessary ways. It is also why we are $15 trillion dollars in national debt and counting, approximately $62 trillion in Medicare debt, and over $11 million in Social Security debt. All this is because of poor judgment, lack of control, and no regard for American wage earners by the elected politicians in Washington. This should make you so angry you will be compelled to take action. Just hold on, we'll show you how at the end.

"Governments view of the economy could be summed up in a few short phrases: If it moves, tax it. If it keeps moving, regulate it. And if it stops moving, subsidize it."

Ronald Reagan

CHAPTER 3
Why We Don't Need the IRS

A No Brainer chapter in good ole' American common sense

As an American that loves your country, are you concerned at the direction this country is going and the utter lack of accountability you witness every day from your elected officials in Washington?

Do you find yourself rolling your eyes in disbelief at the lack of the most basic common sense exhibited by the 545 elected leaders running this nation?

Would you vote to restore common sense, accountability, and solutions that work for the everyday, hard working American like yourself? Would it feel good to be able to look at Washington with a sense of pride and honor?

FACT #1

THE IRS IS NOT SUSTAINABLE

When Charles Rossotti retired as the IRS Commissioner, he said, "The IRS is losing the war against tax cheats." Subsequent studies confirmed his fears. It has only gotten worse each year.

What started with a few minor cheaters has grown into a massive number of major ones. There are now literally millions of non-tax filers, criminals, crooks, and thieves. It seems a lot of Americans, both legal and illegal, are using the politicians in Washington as role models.

The IRS is unsustainable for the following common sense reasons:

1. The Federal budget keeps growing every year.
2. More and more government "give away" (social-ist) programs to lazy, *legal* citizens.
3. More and more government "give away" pro-gram to millions of *illegal* aliens.
4. Congress continues to delete more and more "special interest" taxpayers from paying right-ful taxes.
5. More and more tax evasion.
6. More and more wage earners who do not file.
7. Too few honest tax paying Americans who are paying 238% more taxes annually because of the above.

Why? Simply because an out of touch, irresponsi-ble Congress has refused to close down this broken IRS nightmare and come up with a simple, common sense alternative (See chapter 4).

FACT #2

IT NOW COSTS MORE FOR THE AMERICAN TAXPAYER AND CORPO-RATE BUSINESS TAXPAYERS TO *PRE-PARE* THEIR ANNUAL TAXES *THAN ALL THE TAXES THE IRS COLLECTS EACH YEAR*

WHERE IS THE COMMON SENSE IN THAT?

Take a look on the next page at the actual tax col-lections and refunds by type of tax for fiscal year 2010. The CFO of Revenue Financial Management U.S. Gov-ernment supplied this information.

Net Collections and Refunds, by Type of Income Tax,

Fiscal Year 2010:

Type of Tax	Revenue Generated
United States, total	$1,877,753,005,000
Individual income	$814,015,326,000
Business income tax	$179,598,611,000
Estate and trust income tax	$8,759,011,000
Estate tax	$16,115,899,000
Gift tax	$2,726,869,000

The above taxes cost over four billion hours of time for American individuals in tax preparation. Multiply those four billion hours times $30 average per hour and you come up to $1,200,000,000,000. This does *not* include the cost for all American businesses and corporations in America. Major corporations often have a stack of tax forms reaching eight to ten feet high.

Paul Damazo with a stack of tax forms for one major American corporation.

Imagine the cost of corporate tax preparation. We are talking hundreds of thousands of dollars for one major corporation. And we still have not counted the cost of crating and shipping it to the IRS.

What ever happened to common sense?

> I have wondered at times about what the Ten Commandments would have looked like if Moses had run them through the U.S. Congress.

FACT #3

THE AVERAGE HONEST AMERICAN TAXPAYER PAYS INCOME TAXES SIX WAYS.

1. Sixty-one percent of Americans have to *pay professional tax preparers,* which can run into thousands of dollars because tax filing is so complicated.
2. Then there is the cost to pay the actual taxes to the IRS.
3. Then you pay the cost of business and corporate tax preparation. Don't be duped. Corporations just add their tax cost to their product. When you purchase it, you pay for the business and corporate taxes as well.
4. Honest taxpayers pay 238% more in taxes due to the tens of millions of non-filers and non-payers.
5. You pay your extra share of taxes to cover the cost of IRS administration, enforcement, record keeping, tax filing advice and collection.
6. The majority of taxpayers over pay unintentionally due to the complicated tax code. This is because most choose to play it "safe" in their deductions rather than suffer the nightmare of an IRS audit.

Another reason we do not need the IRS is because it is simply not accurate. Callers to the IRS seeking answers to their questions are given wrong answers *seventy-five percent of the time.* Yet the IRS takes no blame. And you are held responsible.

National statistics show the IRS is run so badly that nearly half of the thirty-six million notices it sends out each year demanding additional taxes or penalties are incorrect. Blame it on the politicians in Washington. They have created a tax code that is an incomprehensible mess, playing into the hands of fraudulent promoters and cheats.

A New Word in the Dictionary

Ineptocracy (In-ep-toc"-ra-cy)- A system of government where the least capable lead, and where the members of society least likely to sustain themselves or succeed are rewarded with goods and services paid for by the confiscated wealth of a diminishing number of producers.

FACT #4

The IRS mission statement is a total lie.
IRS MISSION STATEMENT
"TO PROVIDE AMERICAN TAX PAYERS TOP QUALITY SERVICE BY HELPING THEM UNDERSTAND AND MEET THEIR TAX RESPONSIBILITY AND BY APPLYING THE TAX WITH INTEGRITY AND FAIRNESS TO ALL."

Let's review this mission statement a section at a time.

1. **"To provide American tax payers top quality service."**

A.   Have you tried calling the IRS lately?
       How long did you have to wait? The
       angels of heaven would have to blush
       if I put on paper the remarks people
       give me when I ask that question.
B.   How many recordings did you get?
       How many in English?
C.   Half of the thirty-six million notices
       sent out each year are incorrect.
       How's that for quality service?

2. **"By helping them understand..."**
   A.   How can they help when *no one in
          America* can understand the tax code,
          including the IRS agents themselves?
   B.   Not even the IRS commissioner under-
          stands the total tax code.
   C.   As stated earlier, seventy-five percent
          of all callers to the IRS received wrong
          information.

3. **"Fairness to all."** Are you rolling on the floor
   while hysterically gasping for breath by now?
   Somebody is smoking something stronger than
   Marlboros. *Fair?*
   A.   The top 2.5% of taxpayers paid forty-
          two percent of all income tax collected.
   B.   The top 10% of taxpayers paid 61% of
          all federal income tax.
   C.   The bottom 64% pay only 15% per-
          cent.
   D.   The bottom 40% paid less than 1%
          percent.
   E.   Fifty-four million do not pay any tax at
          all.
   F.   Multiple millions do not even file a tax

return, including nearly all the illegal aliens.

Is this what you call "fairness for all?" How stupid does the IRS think you are?

The politicians in Washington alone are responsible. They should be held accountable by their bosses: You and I.

CHAPTER 4
The Alternative to the IRS – An Exceedingly Simple 10% National Sales Tax

As an over stressed American so busy trying to survive, do you long for less stress and a more simple life?

Do you ever feel that the "American Dream" will never happen to you?

Would you be willing to take five minutes of your time to cast a vote online—and by doing so help eliminate the single biggest time and money waster in your life?"

THERE IS ONLY *ONE ALTERNATIVE.* CONGRESS AND THE PRESIDENT MUST CLOSE DOWN THE IRS.
THE SIMPLE SOLUTION
A SIMPLE NATIONAL 10% SALES TAX FOR ALL AMERICANS.
THIS IS *ALL* WE NEED
THIS SIMPLE NATIONAL 10% SALES TAX WOULD BE ADDED TO ALL PURCHASES MADE AT THE RETAIL LEVEL ON ALL GOODS AND SERVICES, EXCEPT EDUCATION AND MEDICAL PURCHASES.
IT IS THAT SIMPLE.

The government would collect the ten percent National Sales Tax by contracting with the fifty states (forty-six already collect state taxes). This plan could be implemented in less than a week. The government would pay States the cost of collecting the National Sales Tax. The U.S. Treasury would be in charge.

NOTE: Please do not be fooled with the number of "alternate systems" to *replace* the IRS, like the "Flat Tax" or "VAT Tax." They are anything but simple. Many of these alternate plans are more complicated than what we currently have. We do not want to *"replace"* the IRS; we want to END it.

Let's take a look now at the beauty, simplicity, and common sense of a National Sales Tax.

WHO PAYS THIS TAX?

EVERYONE. All Americans are now equal, as our Constitution guarantees. Everyone who purchases anything new on the retail level, except for education and medical purchases, will pay.

Wait a minute! I can hear some of you saying, "You mean the poor, Warren buffet and Bill Gates are all going to pay the same 10% National Sales Tax?" Yes, they will. Rather than Congress and IRS mandating their amount, *each individual* determines how much "tax" they end up paying, based on their purchases.

The wealthy naturally purchase anywhere from 25 to 100 times more than do the poor. So they will be paying 25 to 100 more taxes than do the poor. Right now the top 2.5% of all taxpayers pay forty-two percent of all the individual income tax paid. That is not honest or fair. The National Sales Tax would make it fair for all.

The bottom forty percent of all taxpayers pay less than one percent of all income tax, but receive eighty percent of all government services on all levels of government. This is terribly unfair. Again the National Sales Tax would make everyone equal.

It is time for America to be honest. The rich, middle class and poor all utilize the same excellent roads, bridges, drinking water, fire and police services and armed forces. Thus, it is only right and fair that every American pay their share.

And yes, that includes the healthy poor. The healthy poor do not need government handouts. This only demeans them, fosters their problem, and makes them dependent without taking responsibility. They need to be inspired to come out of poverty and do their part to contribute to this great land.

American healthy poor don't know what poverty is. I've been to nearly every country of the world, and our healthy poor are incredibly rich if compared to the real poor of the world. Every day you to live in America, you ought to kiss the hallowed ground and thank your Creator that you have the privilege to live in this great country.

Yes, there are *worthy poor.* And it is our privilege and honor to care for those who suffer from mental or physical disabilities, or who cannot care for themselves. But that represents a *very small percentage of our population.*

The first study done on the effects of gambling in the U.S. showed that the poor, on government welfare and food stamps, purchased the majority of the weekly lottery tickets. They spent an average of $599 per year. If they can waste their money like that, certainly they can pay 10% National Sales Tax on their purchases.

It is one thing to be poor. But you don't have to stay poor. Both of us writing this book had immigrant parents who came to America with nothing. Paul's parents had ten children before and during the great depression. They taught them that *the two most important things in life were get an education and do an honest day's work.*

By the third grade all seven boys were earning (during the Depression) enough money to pay for school tuition at a private Christian school, as well as to pay for their own clothing. Three of the ten became doctors, one with a Master's degree and the rest were college graduates. All ten children earned 100% of their schooling from the third grade on. They all worked 100% of their way through school, including board, room, clothing, transportation, etc., and all graduated *debt free*. The family knew what it was like to be poor and they determined to work their way out of it. (By the way, five of the seven boys went on to become multimillionaires and well known philanthropists.) No American has to stay poor.

GREAT NEWS FOR CORPORATIONS AND SMALL BUSINESS THAT MAKE AMERICA WORK

In the National Sales Tax, 100% of all the business and corporate income tax will be eliminated (See chapter 6). Do you have any idea what benefit this will have for you as an American? Don't forget these businesses and corporations that pay income tax add it directly to the cost of their products. This means when you purchase anything, you are paying *their* taxes as well. That is costing you a lot of money.

But if corporations and small business do not have to pay up to 35% federal tax, plus substantial state taxes, or if they no longer have to spend money on preparing hundreds of tax forms, they will be able to lower their prices significantly. Remember that America runs on competition. Nearly all goods and services will become much cheaper. *Therefore, in many cases, the ten percent National Sales Tax you pay could end up zero because of the substantial reduced cost and lower retail prices.*

NOW *THAT* IS GOOD OLE' COMMON AMERICAN SENSE.

WILL THE TEN PERCENT NATIONAL SALES TAX BE ADEQUATE TO RE-PLACE IRS COLLECTED INCOME TAX?

Please refer to the next illustration below to see the actual amount of income tax collected by the IRS for 2010.

COLLECTION BY TYPE OF TAX (FISCAL YEAR 2010)

$814,015,326,000	Individual Income Tax
$179,598,611,000	Business Income Tax
$ 8,759,011,000	Estate & trust income Taxes
$16,115,899,000	Estate or death tax (One and the same)
$2,726,868,000	Gift taxes
$1,021,215,715,000	Total

Total income taxes collected from individuals, business, plus (estate or death) gift tax for 2010 tax year. So just remember the figure: *One Trillion, Twenty one billion* collected in tax from the IRS.

Source: Chief financial officer, Revenue Financial Management, U. S. Government

NOW LOOK AT THE NATIONAL SALES TAX

Total personal purchases made in 2010*

$10,245,000,000,000

*Source: U.S. Department of Commerce Bureau of Economic Analysis.
Income from 10% national sales tax.

$1,024,000,000,000

Now, remember this figure,

One trillion, twenty four billion with a National Sales Tax.

This leaves a Surplus of: *$ 2,784,283,000*

MORE REVENUE IS GENERATED WITH A SIMPLE 10% NATIONAL SALES TAX THAN THE IRS IS CURRENTLY COLLECTING!

This surplus can help America begin to pay off its national debt. But we need more to pull out of the insane debt our elected leaders have created.

SO LET'S LOOK AT TWO MAJOR *ADDITIONAL* SOURCES OF INCOME TAX TO HELP GET OUT OF DEBT.

#1. The Top 1% of Salary Earners:

The U.S. government recently reported the following:

1. The top 1% of American households saw their incomes soar 275% in the last 28 years.
2. Sixty percent of middle class households saw their incomes go up only 40%
3. The lowest 20% of households saw their income go up only 18% during the same time.

The top 1%, who have increased 275%, are primarily the "superstar" actors, athletes, musicians, and corporate executives.

At this point we need to discuss something very

important. We believe very strongly in the American entrepreneur spirit, and that *small business and corporations are in business to make money and should never be punished for doing so.* Taxing the small business or large corporations more than others is not constitutional. If they are taxed more, they simply pass it on to the American people. This is why you *never want to tax "wealthy business corporations."*

THIS IS A CRUCIAL POINT: MEMORIZE IT!

But, when a CEO of a bank that was bailed out with your tax money is proven to be a completely incompetent businessman, and yet draws a salary of $7 million a year, we know something is wrong. An athlete who is paid $26 million for a 4-year contract while the typical salary for the other players is 1/10 of what the super-athlete earns is unique. A 16-year-old kid who becomes a teen idol overnight and is making $30 million a year is in a different category than most musicians. This is the 1% of *personal income earners* we are talking about. We are not talking about the wealthy corporations. This, again, is a crucial distinction.

Should this 1% pay an additional tax?

I've talked to a lot of these men and women. And you know what? Most of them are the nicest, most giving Americans you will ever meet. They know they are fortunate and blessed. And most of them give large amounts of their money away each year to causes, anyway. I would bet that 98% of them would be happy to pay an extra 10% tax each year to help America get back on its feet and out of debt.

AS A RESULT, WE ARE PROPOSING AN ADDITIONAL 10% SURTAX ON ALL

PERSONAL INCOME EARNERS OF 2 ½ MILLION DOLLARS OR MORE A YEAR

This is only logical. Let's take my doctor friend, who went to school for 25 plus years. He earns only about $220,000 a year and yet saves hundreds of lives each year. Along comes a sixteen-year-old who can sing, and by age twenty-five has earned more money than my doctor will ever earn in a lifetime. We are proud of the teen, good for him, and chances are he will gladly pay an extra 10%.

The media has really mixed up this issue and put the two issues as one. Don't fall for it. Keep the two separate.

Corporate and small business profit should never be punished or taxed higher.

Personal income from the top 1% of people who are exceptionally blessed with a salary of 2 ½ million a year or more should be happy to pay an extra 10%. That is the American spirit.

#2. Government Employees:

The majority of federal employees are in a different universe when it comes to wages, benefits, job responsibility, and lifetime employment. A government employee typically receives twenty percent more income than the same comparable employee in a non-federal government job, plus they retire earlier and many retirees receive an exceedingly high salary during retirement. This imbalance is not constitutional. We propose that all government employees on all levels should have all wages and benefits reduced by 15%, including all government retirees.

Civilian employees all across the nation are taking pay cuts. Government employees should bear some of the responsibility as well.

> "To preserve our independents we must not let our leaders load us with perpetual debt."
> Thomas Jefferson

IN SUMMARY

1. Congress needs to pass a Balanced Budget Amendment.
2. Congress needs to repeal the 16th Amendment.
3. Congress and the President need to shut down the IRS now. It can never be fixed.
4. The IRS needs to be replaced with an exceedingly simple 10% National Sales Tax, with no exceptions except education and medical purchases.
5. Stop pork barrel spending.
6. No more hidden taxes added.
7. No new government programs until all fraud and waste are eliminated on existing programs. This is hundreds of billions of dollars each year.
8. Reduce all of free government programs from 19,000 to 500.

WHY THE TEN PERCENT NATIONAL SALES TAX WILL WORK

It will create more taxes than the net amount the IRS brings in now. Why? Because *everyone* will be paying the 10% National Sales Tax when they make purchases. This includes:

1. The millions of non-filers.

2. The 54,000,000 non-taxpayers.
3. The "underground" non-taxpayers.
4. American tax cheats.

Criminals, drug dealers, money launderers, prostitutes, etc., all have one thing in common. They do not pay income tax. We have been paying their share along with the tens of millions of others. The great news is,

ALL OF THE ABOVE WILL BE PAYING THE TEN PERCENT NATIONAL SALES TAX.

Once and for all we will have a fair tax where everyone pays.

NOW, WE NEED 33 MILLION OF YOU TO TAKE ACTION. RIGHT NOW. WHEREVER YOU ARE. GO TO www.closetheirsnow.com AND DO *THREE THINGS.*

VOTE. It counts.

Invest $10.00 to help us get this through Congress.

Tell everyone you know, and have them vote and contribute $10.00

"Why can't Americans do their own taxes? Because the Federal Tax Code is out of control, that is why. It is gigantic and insanely complex, and it gets worse all the time. Nobody has ever read the whole thing. IRS workers are afraid to go into the same room with it." Dave Barry

CHAPTER 5
THE ADVANTAGES AND BENEFITS TO AMERICAN CITIZENS IN CLOSING DOWN THE IRS

You are one of over three hundred million Americans. Maybe you are a dad, a mom, grandparent, business owner, student or employee. Do your financial dreams and hopes seem impossible?

Financial stress is the number one cause of divorce, child abuse and spousal abuse in the USA. Are you sick of the stress?

We can begin to turn that around today by showing you the benefits of closing down the IRS, and the peace and freedom it will bring to your life and family. All you have to do is read, and then go to the website and vote one time at: *www.closetheirsnow.com*

One of the great days in American history will be the day the IRS is closed down. The celebration will be a combination of July 4th, Thanksgiving Day and New Year's Eve all rolled into one glorious event. Advantages will be:

1. A well deserved day of stress relief for the American people.
2. Tens of billion of hours of time will be saved by individual Americans, businessmen and corporations.
3. All 313 million Americans will be paying their fair share of taxes including all the liars, cheaters, and illegals.
4. You will pay only 10% tax on all your retail purchases.

5. The 10% National Sales Tax is the simplest of all alternatives being advocated.

6. Forty-six states already collect tax. It would be very simple for U.S. Treasury to contract with all fifty states to collect the National 10% Sales Tax.

7. No IRS, or tens of thousands of pages of tax code ever needed again.

8. So simple. The new system takes only four words to explain.

YOU BUY, YOU PAY

9. No deductions and loopholes of any kind. Every person is treated the same.

10. An immediate and powerful impact on the level of economic activity. America's international competitiveness will increase immediately. There are thousands of books, studies, and case examples to prove this true.

11. A radical shift in the American mind from consumption to investing.

12. American citizens may earn as much as they choose without being punished.

"The question is: What can we, as citizens, do to reform our tax system? As you know, under three-branch system of government, the tax laws are created by: SATAN. But he works through the Congress, so that is where we must focus our efforts."

Dave Barry.

NO MORE:

Tax records, deductions, filing, April 15, letters from the IRS, tax cheats, tax loopholes, off shore tax havens, tax lobbying, time wasted by Congress working on tax matters, tax audits, Income taxes to pay, Trust income tax to pay, Gift taxes, Estate or death tax, Inheritance tax, Business tax, hidden corporate taxes of any kind, Capital gains tax, tax on savings, tax on all investments, loopholes in exchange for political support and favors, and criminal activity incentives (like Enron's 320 illegal partnerships that hid income).

BENEFITS FOR THE AMERICAN PEOPLE:

1. Increased jobs, increased standard of living, improved civil liberties, ability to maintain more of your privacy, and no more tax advice, which means less personal expense.
2. More money will be collected from the National 10% Sales Tax compared to what the IRS collects in net income taxes from individuals, business and corporations combined. This will help pay our national debt. (We really should pass a law that the leaders in Washington are responsible for this debt and we will garnish 70% of their wages till it is paid off.)
3. No more need for business and corporations to move overseas to avoid U.S. income tax. In fact, there will be a massive relocation of companies back to U.S. providing trillions of dollars in cash flow and hundreds of thousands of new U.S. jobs.
4. The underground economy will not go away completely, but it will be curbed greatly.
5. Everyone in the USA will have to pay the 10%

tax. This is huge for our economy. A few examples are:

People who hire people and pay cash illegally will now be paying.

Non-filers will now be paying.

54 million Americans that do not have to file a tax return will now pay their fair share.

Prostitutes, handymen, maids and all other vocations that are often paid cash under the table will now pay their share.

All those citizens holding *$12 trillion dollars in many parts of the world* to avoid U.S. income tax will now be paying 10% like the rest of us. As a side benefit, these trillions of dollars will start flowing back to the U.S. because there is no benefit to keeping it offshore any longer.

Money launderers will have to pay.

Drug dealers will have to pay.

Illegal aliens would have to pay.

6. The U.S. would become the world's tax haven due to our financial status. International business would flock to the USA, providing more jobs and cash flow.

7. You would have freedom to grow your own money with any investment you desire but with no income tax consequences. This would be the greatest "stimulus" package ever seen by American citizens.

8. Americans would be free to keep their estate tax, and free to pass on your estate at death with NO TAX CONSEQUENCES.

9. How about USA exporters? They would no longer be taxed twice since exports are consumed overseas.

Think about it this way. How much will you spend on taxes this year, and how much will you pay to have someone prepare your taxes? Take $10 of that money and invest it with us, vote, and think how much you will save once we abolish the IRS. Go to www.closetheirsnow.com and tell everyone else you know!

"And to you taxpayers out there, let me say this: make sure you file your tax return on time and re-member that, even though income taxes can be a pain in the neck, the folks at the IRS are regular people just like you, except that they can destroy your life."

Dave Barry.

CHAPTER 6
WHY ALL BUSINESS AND CORPORATE TAXES SHOULD BE ELIMINATED NOW

Small business in America
- Represent 99.7 percent of all employer firms
- Employ half of all private sector employees
- Pay 44 percent of total U.S. private payroll
- Generated 65 percent of net new jobs
- Create more than half of the nonfarm private GDP
- Hire 43 percent of high tech workers
- Are 52 percent home-based and 2 percent franchises
- Make up 97.5 percent of all exports
- Produce $31 billion in revenue

This represents most of you as an owner or employee. But the IRS is crushing small business with taxes. The joy of being a business owner has now been replaced with the discouragement of the IRS taking away any incentive to make a profit. Would you like to see a change where you could enjoy business again? Where you could keep more of your hard earned profits? A way to free up more of your time to build your business and enjoy the rewards?

Congress is so deceitful in so many ways that taxpayer's cup of anger and wrath is ready to spill over. Especially when you really understand what they are doing to small business.

While this affects you as an American, it has an even more disastrous effect on the most important part of American economy— the corporate and small business owners who employ Americans and keep this country working.

FOR DECADES THE CONGRESS, THROUGH THE IRS, HAS LEVIED HIGH BUSINESS AND CORPORATE INCOME TAXES. THESE TAXES WERE PLANNED AS A MAJOR COVER-UP TO COLLECT LARGE SUMS OF ADDITIONAL FUNDS.

When the government began to do this, very few American taxpayers realized what was happening. Immediately, corporate income taxes collected by the IRS increased about 40%. Congress knew it was pulling the wool right over the taxpayers' eyes when it passed the diabolical business and corporate tax. The sad thing is that the average American knows very little about how business and corporation finances work, much less their income tax system.

"When there is a single thief, it is robbery. When there are a thousand thieves, it's taxation."
Vanya Cohen

THE PROBLEM

Business and corporations in essence do not pay income tax. The real truth is that the majority of business corporations are merely collection agents for the IRS. Yes, they pay taxes, but they simply add the tax and cost directly onto the cost of their products. You buy, and you pay their taxes. It should make you mad.

There are hundreds of these hidden taxes that the average American is not aware of day by day. This is why all business and corporate taxes should be eliminated now.

The U.S. is the only westernized country that still has business and corporate taxes.

And, it is killing our economy. Here is what is happening. If a small business or corporation is paying up to 35% federal tax, plus state income tax, they simply add that to their product price. So automatically their product is 35% higher that their international competitor. The result is more lost jobs and business for all Americans.

Many U.S. companies have moved 100% of their operations overseas, just to avoid state tax and up to 35% federal income tax. More jobs lost again.

Many other companies that have not closed down their U.S. operations have subsidiaries overseas for the same reasons.

Many of these companies maintain their profits overseas to eliminate U.S. taxes.

As a result, it has been estimated that between *1 ½ and 2 trillion dollars are kept overseas* by U. S. corporations.

WHAT ARE THE EFFECTS?

Reduced competitiveness.

Continuous loss of U.S. jobs.

Tremendous loss of capital which could be brought back and used in U.S. to expand, build buildings, be more competitive, create more jobs, and stimulate the economy.

CONGRESS IS DEAD WRONG!

By maintaining a business and corporate income tax, the leaders of the country are bringing our country to its knees. It is time to stop it. Remember, it costs American companies more to *prepare* their tax returns than the IRS collects. That is an insane fact.

SUMMARY

1. EVERY AMERICAN NEEDS TO BE AWARE OF THE FRAUD PERPETUATED BY CONGRESS AND THE IRS, WHICH IS: *BUSINESS AND CORPORATIONS DO NOT PAY INCOME TAX.* THEY MERELY COLLECT AND PASS IT ON TO THE IRS. YOU, THE AMERICAN CITIZEN, PAYS THE TAX.

2. THE CONGRESS AND IRS ARE RESPONSIBLE FOR LARGE NUMBERS OF LOST U.S. JOBS.

3. THE CONGRESS AND IRS ARE RESPONSIBLE FOR A SUBSTANTIAL LOSS OF U.S. INTERNATIONAL COMPETITIVENESS.

4. THIS FRAUD CONTINUES, YEAR AFTER YEAR, WHILE THE PROBLEMS BECOME GREATER EACH YEAR.

6. IT IS TIME TO FORCE THE PRESIDENT AND CONGRESS TO UNDERSTAND WHAT THEY ARE DOING TO OUR NATION AS WE SEE MORE AND MORE CORPORATIONS FLEE AMERICA LIKE RATS FROM A SINKING SHIP WHILE AMERICANS LOSE JOBS, COMPETITIVENESS AND LARGE SUMS OF CAPITAL.

CHAPTER 7
WHY THE FLAT TAX SHOULD NOT BE CONSIDERED

Have you ever sat in front of your TV, watching CNN and saying to yourself, "Is it possible to find a more incompetent, out of touch group of people on earth than what we have in Washington?"

How many times have you rolled your eyes and said, "What kind of morons are running this country?"

How would you like to start to exercise those feelings and take control of Washington? How would you feel knowing you were finally able to use your common sense to run this country? My fellow American, you can. It all starts by your vote. After this chapter, let your voice be heard by voting online at: *www.closetheirsnow.com*. You will bring common sense back to Washington.

Lets begin with some common sense regarding the flat tax.

The flat income tax system can simply be described as a combination of the current tax system with an added flat tax. There are multiple versions being proposed, a true flat tax, a marginal flat tax, a modified flat tax, etc.

There are a number of flat tax promoters, and they all vary with their flat tax option, but at the core they are the same: *a combination of our current messed up system with an added flat tax.*

The concept is simply wrong, just another complicated mess created by Washington bureaucrats. The same gangsters, tax cheats, dead beats and the 54 million non-filers who are escaping current taxes will escape the flat tax as well.

THE DISADVANTAGES OF THE FLAT TAX SYSTEM

1. It does not eliminate the IRS. The 10% National Sales Tax gets rid of the IRS completely.
2. Most flat tax plans require a combination of the existing IRS income tax code, plus a high flat tax. Translation: more nightmares than you already have. The 10% National Sales Tax ends all your nightmares.
3. A flat tax is just one more complication added to an already crazily complicated IRS system. You need fewer headaches, not more. The 10% National Sales Tax eliminates all your tax headaches.
4. Why even have a flat tax? With the national 10% sales tax, everything is eliminated.
5. The flat tax is not fair to all Americans. The 10% National Sales Tax treats everyone equal and fair.
6. The government is required in some flat tax systems to print tens of millions of refund checks every month. In most cases, refunds and credits are ongoing for low-income people. The current IRS mission states: "taxes are fair to everyone." Giving substantial monthly government checks partly because some families have children is not fair. Americans are not against children; however, I do not feel it is my neighbors and other taxpayer's responsibility to pay higher taxes to support or even help to

support my children. My children are my responsibility.

Having children is the decision of a man and a woman only, and not the government or anyone else. No one has the right to have children and expect taxpayers to work longer hours and pay more taxes to support them. Congressmen and government workers on all levels have no business creating laws that encourages people to have children because they are going to get a free check at your expense.

The government, colleges, universities, and churches should be teaching individual responsibility. You should not have children you cannot support. The 10% National Sales Tax will eliminate this horrific lack of accountability and responsibility.

7. Most versions of the flat tax favors imports while hurting our exports. The 10% National Sales Tax will massively increase our exports.

8. The flat tax requires individual tax reporting. The 10% National Sales Tax will end reporting forever.

9. In the flat tax, the IRS would still audit you. The 10% National Sales Tax will eliminate all audits forever.

10. The flat tax would still encourage companies to move completely or partially overseas to avoid taxes. A 10% National Sales Tax will keep companies in in the US.

11. Jobs would still be leaving the US. A 10% National Sales Tax will create millions of new jobs in the US.

12. With a flat tax, the IRS would still be involved with tax collection. The 10% National Sales

Tax dissolves the IRS.

My fellow Americans, we have *only 5 options.*

Take one minute and figure it out.

Option 1. Keep the existing, broken down, irreparable, unfair, crooked tax system, which is not sustainable.

Option 2. Add a Flat tax, making the current system even more complicated and time consuming.

Option 3. Add a Value added tax (VAT), which will only add more laws and regulations (see next chapter).

Option 4. There are a few other options created by politicians that make no sense worth mentioning.

Option 5. Abolish the IRS completely and go to a super simple, fair for all Americans, 10% National Sales tax. *It is so simple you can explain it in four words: YOU BUY, YOU PAY.*

"A fool and his money is soon parted. It takes creative tax laws for the rest."

Bob Chaces

CHAPTER 8
WHY THE VALUE-ADDED TAX (VAT) SHOULD *NOT* BE CONSIDERED

You are a patriotic American, right? You believe in the principles of life, liberty and the pursuit of happiness. But you are fed up with how the leaders in Washington are trying to turn America in to a socialist country like Europe. Are you filled with indignation that your government wants to turn this great county your forefathers died for into a welfare state? Can you believe we have come to a point where government leaders would even consider a VAT tax?

We are not Europe, or Canada. We are Americans. We told the British a long time ago we did not want their system. I'm calling you back to that spirit of independence, that attitude of pride in our constitution, and that freedom only we Americans know and love.

The value-added tax's *ONLY PURPOSE IS TO IN-CREASE GOVERNMENT INCOME.* Why should we give these Washington politicians more money when they have proven they are no more fiscally responsible than a two year old? Why give them more money when they have put us trillions in debt already?

The VAT tax is used as *an added tax* in the production and distribution of goods and services, basically a "consumption or sales" tax.

The value added tax (VAT) is the most devilish, complicated, costly options of all tax alternatives. It would take a couple of books to cover the basic variations and complications of the value added tax.

Some would argue that it has been in use for decades in some countries, and so should be an option for the U.S. But the U.S. has the most worthless, diabolical, complicated tax system in the world, and the VAT option *combines the horrific U.S. tax system with another incredibly complicated value-added tax.*

The value-added tax has multiple inclusions, exclusions, direct and indirect taxes on income, dozens of term definitions, side issues, various types of taxes on goods and services, registrations, indirect taxes, credits, trade barriers, etc.

If Congress were to leave the existing tax system as is, and add the value-added tax (VAT) to increase government revenue, the Boston Tea Party, which was an insurrection, would reoccur again. The president, Congress and the IRS would have an instant revolt on their hands.

OTHER DISADVANTAGES OF THE VALUE-ADDED TAX

1. It does nothing to make the government more efficient and effective to require less income. It gives the politicians more of your money to spend.
2. It is the most hideous of all options being considered.
3. It is the most complicated of all options.
4. It would be the most costly to implement and maintain.
5. It would not do away with the IRS.
6. IRS audits would still be required.
7. It would not do away with our current broken tax system.
8. Where it is used it is almost always used with a personal income tax system.
9. It will make international trade more difficult.

10. It has one purpose only: *to get more money out of our pockets.* Americans forget that all government workers from the federal, state, counties and cities are employees or servants of all the American citizens. THEY WORK FOR YOU AND ME. WE TELL THEM WHAT TO DO. NEVER FORGET THAT.

Keep value-added tax or VAT out of America. It is not the solution. The only solution is a 10% National Sales Tax.

Cast your vote at: www.closetheirsnow.com.

"GIVING MONEY AND POWER TO GOVERNMENT IS LIKE GIVING WHISKEY AND CAR KEYS TO TEENAGE BOYS."
P. J. O'ROURKE

CHAPTER 9
REDUCE GOVERNMENT WASTE AND FRAUD

Do you find yourself being careful how you spend your money over the last few years? Maybe you decided not to take that vacation, or buy something you need because you feel uneasy about your financial future?

At the same time are you irritated at a government that takes half your hard earned money in taxes, and then spends it with no accountability or reason?

Would you like to see Washington held accountable? Would you like to see the trillions of dollars the government wastes come back to your pocket? It can happen if you take action.

WOULD YOU BELIEVE THAT EVERY DOLLAR THE U.S. GOVERNMENT SPENDS, FORTY-TWO CENTS COMES FROM BORROWED MONEY?

No person, no family, no business, and no government can continue borrowing this shocking amount of money and get by with without something blowing up.

Our irresponsible president and Congress have put our country into this horrible condition with a $15,000,000,000,000 national debt and increasing at the rate of 1 ½ trillion dollars more each year. Add to that an estimated $62 trillion Medicare debt and an estimated $11 trillion Social Security debt, and you begin to realize what the government has done to you.

But—guess what? You and I are to blame too. American apathy has allowed them to do this. But, if you want things to change, you have to be heard. So, if you have not voted yet online, go right now to: www.closetheirsnow.com and vote.

At this rate we are quickly becoming a third world nation, losing our national security and our standard of living. For all practical purposes, we are bankrupt. Yet almost every time our president speaks, he announces a new spending program.

Americans pay between $.50 to $.57 per dollar of wages on income taxes, which includes hundreds of hidden taxes. Yet the government is always looking for additional sources of revenue. SO, THE PROBLEM IS NOT CONTINUING TO FIND NEW SOURCES OF REVENUE, BUT TO REDUCE SPENDING RAPIDLY.

Tens of millions of Americans are sick and tired of this, and we are on the verge of a revolt. We are sick and tired of watching our beloved America become the laughing stock of the world. And we are uniting to change it.

THE IMMEDIATE SOLUTION?

REDUCE GOVERNMENT SPENDING, WASTE AND FRAUD

There are a few dedicated, conservative Congressmen who are working on this phenomenally important project now. We invite you to join us and add these items to your list of cost reductions to implement now.

1. **Citizens Against Government Waste** is an outstanding organization. They released an urgent, special report that lists 700 specific government spending programs amounting to $360,000,000,000 per year for five years amounting to $1.8 trillion dollar savings in just five years. It is shocking and discouraging to read this list of 700 wasteful, unnecessary, and needless items. It should be mandatory that all politicians and the president go to *www.cagw.org* and read this list. Just think, three hundred and sixty billion per year for five years is $1.8 trillion!

2. The U.S. Government accountability office has a new book entitled "Opportunities in Government Programs, Save Tax Dollars and Enhance Revenue." This book contains 340 pages. Again, this should be mandatory reading for the president and all politicians in Washington. And it should be mandatory to implement everything in the book before any of these members get any vacation or breaks

Take a look at a few recommendations from this book put out by the Government Accountability Office. The following section is on government duplication between the different agency departments for economic development.

Programs by agency

Activity	Commerce	HUD	SBA	USDA	Total
Entrepreneurial efforts	9	12	19	12	52
Infrastructure	4	12	1	18	35
Plans & strategies	7	13	13	6	39
Commercial buildings	4	12	4	7	27
New markets	6	10	6	6	28
Telecommunications	3	11	2	10	26
Business incubators	5	12	-	3	20
Industrial parks	5	11	-	3	19
Tourism	5	10	-	4	19
TOTAL					265

Source: Government Accountability Office (**GAO**)

This is only *one* major disgrace and inefficiency of the U.S. Government. Talk about overlapping, costly and inefficient. Look at the number of agencies handling the same program, a total of 265. That is insane.

Want some more insanity?

There are *fifteen* agencies involved with food safety.

There are *nine* agencies involved just with the water needs in the U.S. Mexico border region.

There are *twenty-four* federal agencies involved with data.

Multiple agencies work on public health information systems.

Seven federal agencies are involved with homelessness.

Eight agencies involved transportation for disadvantaged.

Ten agencies are involved with teacher quality.

Twenty different agencies are involved with financial literacy. No wonder many families and the government are in financial catastrophe!

> Have you ever wondered if both the Democrats and the Republicans are against deficits, WHY DO WE HAVE DEFICITS?

$1.1 billion was paid by USDA farm subsidy payments to more than 170,000 deceased individuals who were receiving automatic monthly deposited funds. GAO stated the reason was because "the agency lacked sufficient management controls." How absurd this one example is. But we all know there are thousands of examples like this. Even the book on page 155 says, "Financial benefits ranging from tens of millions to tens of billions of dollars annually may be realized."

YOUR TAX DOLLARS GO TO *130 SEPARATE PROGRAMS* SERVING THE DISABLED, 72 SAFE-WATER PROGRAMS, AND 132 PROGRAMS SERVING AT-RISK YOUTH.

Chief of Medicare and medical Dr. Donald Berwick recently stated: "Errors, unnecessary care, and other waste my account for about ⅓ of the nearly one trillion dollars a year that tax payers spend on the Medicare program."
MY DEAR FRIEND THAT AMOUNTS TO OVER $333,000,000,000 PER YEAR, AND DOES NOT INCLUDE ALL THE ESTIMATED FRAUD AT $2 BILLION PER MONTH— JUST FROM MEDICARE.

How about stopping the ludicrous payments of subsidies to corporations? Many of these corporations being subsidized earn tens of billions of profit per year.

How about federal salaries? A March 8, 2010 *USA Today* story showed federal employees salaries exceed the private sector pay in 83% of comparable occupations. The median annual salary for a federal worker is 20% more than in the private sector. Federal employees receive automatic wage increases by statute, which provide them with both, "step-up-grade" increase and cost of living adjustments that have exceeded inflation for the past decade. All this while we have 26 million unemployed or underemployed. Many have not only lost their jobs, but also their homes and cars while millions of others have had pay decreases.

We need to reduce pay and benefits by 15% for all federal government workers and retirees on all levels, and 10% for all state and local government workers.

How about holding accountable all the Pork-barrel congressmen? They lose their jobs, with no pensions and benefits, and serve a 5-year jail term for misappropriation of taxpayer money.

You and I do not have the constitutional authority to vote on appropriations. The House of Representatives does.

The Inspector General for taxes of the U.S. Treasury recently reported that "more than 2 million taxpayers, including some prisoners, claiming students as dependents - apparently wrongly received $3.2 billion in college tax credit last year."

We could give thousands of examples, but the point is that we could have trillions more dollars in the treasury if we simply reduced the waste in Washington.

THE SOLUTION

1. No new government programs.
2. All existing government programs audited with private sector inspectors to eliminate all the fraud and corruption in government and save hundreds of billions per year.
3. *Citizens Against Government Waste* are given power to enforce the 700 plus areas of government waste to be implemented in one year. Failure of the politicians to implement these 700 items in one year is an automatic termination of employment, a one million dollar fine per politician and 5 years in jail.
4. The Government Accountability Office is given power to hold accountable the politicians in Washington, who must follow their recommendations for re-structure and efficiency in all areas. To be implemented in one year or all politicians are terminated, fined one million dollars and 5 years in jail.
5. The President and Congress need to be put on a performance/accountability based annual evaluation. If they do not preform the will of the people and the good of the nation, they are fired with no pension or severance pay. If they put America in debt in any area, National, Medicare, or Social Security, they are fined one million dollars and 5 years in jail. It is that simple.
6. Teach our politicians that serving in the presidency, House, or Senate is a privilege, not a free pass for life. A soldier who gives his life fighting for our freedom is to be honored far more than a politician who has put us deep in

debt and has not been true to our constitution. All past and present presidents and politicians should have their salaries capped at $38,000, like the soldier's salary below.

Salary of retired US Presidents
....$180,000 FOR LIFE

Salary of House/Senate
....$174,000 FOR LIFE

Salary of Speaker of the House
....$223,500 FOR LIFE

Salary of Majority/Minority Leaders
.... $193,400 FOR LIFE
    (Plus a gold plated medical plan for life)

Average Salary of Soldier DEPLOYED IN AFGHANISTAN
....$38,000

What's wrong with this picture?

CHAPTER 10
CONGRESS AND IRS ARE ONE OF THE MAIN REASONS FOR OUTSOURCING JOBS AND MONEY

I recently walked across the USA, from Florida to California, in 100 days, ending on my 50th birthday. During this time I talked to many great Americans. I saw the struggle many of them are going through because they lost their jobs, home, or cars and simply can't make ends meet.

Maybe you are one of them, or someone you care about is. You are tired of the stress; you long for the "American Dream." You just wish for an end to the tension and struggle.

Imagine what it would be like to feel secure again. To have a strong nation that supported you and your family and had your best interest in mind—an America that was truly for the people.

How bad do you want that? How much pain are you going to keep going through? If you have had enough, then go to our website and take a stand with us. Go to www.closetheirsnow.com.

THIS CHAPTER IS GOING TO MAKE YOU ANGRY

Americans have known for decades that business, corporations and wealthy Americans have been sending jobs and money out of America to dozens of locations around the world for one main reason: *to avoid or lower their taxes.*

It seems unfathomable that this is so obvious, yet

the politicians in Washington do nothing to stop it. I ask, sincerely: Are these politicians that stupid? Do they simply not care? Are they asleep on the job? What is going on?

> "What this country needs are more unemployed politicians."
>
> Edward Langley, Artist

PROBLEM 1

In the last four decades American business and corporations have been moving all or part of their companies out of the United States to numerous locations around the world to avoid paying income taxes or reduced taxes paid to foreign countries. The numbers were small at first, but now we see a mass exit that continues to accelerate.

THE NUMBER OF BUSINESSES WHO HAVE MOVED OUT OF THE U.S. IS NOW TENS OF THOUSANDS, WITH APPROXIMATELY ONE THOUSAND NEW ONES GOING OVERSEAS EACH YEAR

Why do they go?

To avoid taxes or reduce taxes

To avoid employee benefits or reduce employee benefits

To eliminate health care cost or reduce health care costs

Eliminate or reduce countless, complicated, costly, regulations

The U.S. is the only Westernized country in the

world that has a corporate income tax. That should tell us something. Companies have to stay competitive or close shop. So they go overseas simply to stay in business.

Foreign countries are competing for American corporations to do business with them. Instead of up to 35% maximum federal, plus state tax, many countries offer huge savings that for major corporations amount to *multi-billions of saved tax dollars yearly.*

Many thousands of corporations have moved out of the United States to stay alive. It all boils down to one reason—the OUTDATED U.S. TAX CODE IS FORCING businesses and corporations to flee America.

American Businesses and Corporations pay income tax three ways:

A. They pay a huge amount to prepare income tax returns. For many large corporations the cost of tax preparation is more than what they owe the IRS.

B. Nearly all daily, monthly and annual business decisions are based on income tax consequences at a gigantic operating cost.

C. Businesses pay the actual income tax due.

As stated in Chapter 6, there should be zero taxes on these companies.

ALL THESE AMERICAN CORPORATIONS WANT IS A LEVEL PLAYING FIELD

If they had it their way, they would be back doing business in the United States in a heartbeat. How can our government expect our corporations and businesses to stay here and be competitive when they levy up to 35% federal plus state tax, while our overseas competitors have zero income tax?

PROBLEM 2

The amount of money being held overseas now by American corporations is close to TWO TRILLION DOLLARS AND CLIMBING RAPIDLY YEAR AFTER YEAR.

This money is from profits and saved taxes. What happens to this money? They keep it overseas so they will not have to pay up to 35% if they brought it back to the United States. What do they do with the money overseas? They do like any smart entrepreneur or businessman would do:

1. They create many jobs overseas.
2. Build larger plants.
3. Build new additional plants.
4. Buy out other companies overseas to expand more.

The United States Chamber of Commerce conducted a study and determined that if United States overseas corporations had a ONE TIME tax break and brought $700 billion dollars of profit back home, it would create three million jobs in about two years. This is awesome. But why stop there? We need to eliminate their income tax permanently so these companies and *all* the two trillion dollars would come home. THIS IS WHY YOU HAVE TO VOTE FOR A SIMPLE NATIONAL SALES TAX! If you have not done it so far, go right now to www.closetheirsnow.com and vote your approval.

PROBLEM 3

Only God knows how many millions of great jobs

have left the United States shores for overseas. Right now more new jobs are being created overseas by U.S. corporations than are being created in the United States.

CAN YOU IMAGINE HOW MANY RECOVERED AND NEW JOBS WE WOULD HAVE IN THE UNITED STATES IF THESE THOUSANDS OF COMPANIES ALL CAME HOME WITH THEIR JOBS AND TWO TRILLION DOLLARS?

Plus, we would stop the outflow of almost 1000 new companies a year leaving the United States.

THE ONLY THING STANDING IN THE WAY IS OUR OUTDATED TAX CODE.

These companies would start packing the same day business and corporate taxes were eliminated, and they would come home.

Fellow Americans, I'm just a cowboy from Colorado but I got something called "common sense." So do all of you reading this. This is not rocket science. Compare it to the government solution we recently saw on TV. *A trillion dollars created out of thin air trying to create jobs with fake money.* The result was a spectacular failure. How do the president and Congress come up with such idiocy?

"There seems to be some perverse human characteristic that likes to make things difficult."
Warren Buffet

PROBLEM 4

How would you like to see one million jobs per year

for five years at no cost to tax payers or government?

I have been interested in energy since the 1973 oil embargo to the United States, when we had to sit in our cars for hours to get a tank of gas. Since then, it has been a hobby of mine to stay informed about the energy segment of our economy.

Immediately after the worst financial disaster in U.S. history, when we lost so many millions of jobs so fast, I decided to send a letter with attachments to Energy Secretary Dr. Chew plus 556 personal letters to the president, his cabinet and to all members of the Senate and Congress. Unfortunately they all cared less how many unemployed workers we had. I received only one letter (from Ted Kennedy). It was two pages long and he was very appreciative of my suggestions. He promised to work on it immediately because it was practical, made good sense, and would be highly worthwhile to America. Unfortunately he became sick and died shortly thereafter.

But take a look. This is so simple. One million high-paying *jobs per year* can be added for five years with no cost.

How?

> "I don't make jokes. I just watch
> the government and report the facts."
> Will Rogers

HAVE YOU EVER CONSIDERED HOW MUCH TAX YOU ARE PAYING FOR OIL?

According to the U.S. Department of Labor, America imports twelve million barrels of crude oil *every day* from our enemies or quasi enemies, plus a few friendly nations. This is the main reason for the U.S. ANNUAL TRADE DEFICIT FOR 2010 being $500,070,000,000. (SOURCE: U.S. GOVERNMENT.)

EVERY DOLLAR IN OUR TRADE DEFICIT MEANS ANOTHER DOLLAR OF LOST U.S. LABOR. *BY ELIMINATING THE IMPORTING OF TWELVE MILLION BARRELS OF OIL, WE COULD GENERATE 1,000,000 HIGH PAYING ENERGY JOBS PER YEAR FOR FIVE YEARS.*

According to the U.S. Geological Service study: "We have more oil inside our border than all the other proven oil reserves on earth. Here are the official estimates."

Eight times as much as Saudi Arabia.

Eighteen times as much as Iraq.

Twenty-one times as much as Kuwait.

Twenty-two times as much as Iran.

Five hundred times as much as Yemen.

And it is all here in the U.S.A.

Again, what is the solution our bright and intelligent government comes up with? Ethanol!

I would be remiss by not telling you how absurd the manufacturing of Ethanol is, just to illustrate the idiocy.

1. We do not need it.
2. The U.S. has fuel of various types to last hundreds of years.
3. Ethanol cost more to produce than its sale price. If it weren't for the government subsidizing it with your tax dollars, it would not be on the market. The government is wasting *billions of our tax dollars needlessly* per year that

takes perfect food away from the U.S. and world market. As a result, food prices have increased substantially because of so much grain being diverted.

4. Added Ethanol to our gasoline reduces our MPG.

5. Each plant requires 100 million gallons of water per year. With current and future water shortages in many places, we cannot afford to waste our precious water on a worthless product.

6. We are exporting one billion gallons per year with more planned, while we the taxpayers are *subsidizing* every gallon.

So, there goes more of your tax dollars by our brilliant Congress. America needs to drill it's own oil and create the jobs here.

(See Appendix)

PROBLEM 5

GET OUR OVERSEAS MONEY BACK HOME

Evidently our presidents, Congress, U.S. Treasury and IRS do not realize what the rest of us know. The wealthy have between $10 - $14 trillion US dollars stashed away all around the world for one purpose: *to avoid income tax!*

If we had the simple 10% National Sales Tax, all these wealthy people would be paying their fair share. In addition they would have no need to keep the *twelve trillion dollars overseas.* Consequently all this money would flow home quickly. Just imagine what that would do for our economy! It would give this country a boost as we have never seen in history, in terms of investments and jobs.

Congress needs to pass the 10% National Sales Tax and close down the IRS so all of these things we have been talking about can become a reality.

If these politicians in government were working for the American people instead of kissing the rear ends of corrupt lobbyists, fattening their own pockets and worrying about being reelected, the country would be in good shape.

The good news is—you have the power to change anything you want in Washington. There are tens of millions of Americans who are sick and tired of all this idiocy. All we have to do is unite under one banner. We are committed to see the 10% National Sales Tax succeed.

> "The most pathetic person in the world is someone who has sight,
> but has no vision."
>   Helen Keller

How to Create Millions of New Jobs

1. With a 10% National Sales Tax there would be no need of the average 1000 business and corporations to leave the U.S. annually. This would create and save many jobs.

2. With a 10% National Sales Tax the thousands of U.S. businesses and corporations who are currently overseas would come back home and bring many jobs with them, and add may more new jobs at home.

3. With a 10% National Sales Tax these businesses and corporations would bring back to the U.S. most of the two trillion dollars they have overseas. Can you imagine how this would stimulate our economy?

4. With a 10% National Sales Tax there would be no need of our American wealthy to haven 12 trillion dollars around the world. Can you imagine what 12 trillion dollars would do for our economy, investing and job creation?

5. With a 10% National Sales Tax we would drastically reduce monthly and annual deficit trade imbalance. Every dollar in trade deficit is a dollar of jobs going overseas. Remember, our balance of trade deficit *for the past ten years equaled $561,385,900,000 per year.* Every dollar of this represents U.S. dollars going overseas to create jobs overseas rather than jobs kept in the U.S.

No question, the status quo needs to be changed. Let's do it!

CHAPTER 11

THE EVILS OF CAPITALISM ARE NOT EVIL

If lying were an Olympic event, the Gold would go to the politicians in Washington, the silver to the IRS, and the bronze to the media.

The media in America today makes me gag, especially when it comes to Capitalism. Did you ever notice they never run a story on a great businessman or woman who runs a business based on honesty, ethics, and principle? Do you also realize that these good, ethical businessmen and women make up 99% of our American economy? But no, the Media is focused on that 1% of greedy, dishonest businessmen and women—and so we all get lumped into one bad, nasty camp.

Paul and I have been in business for a combined 90 years. We have been true, ethical, and honest, like 99% of our fellow Americans. The truth is, if you are not honest or ethical, you won't last long in business in America. You will destroy yourself. Americans are not stupid. We reward hard work, ingenuity, creativity, ethics, and honesty. We buy good products and services. If you are not a good business person, Americans won't do business with you any more.

Capitalism is what makes America great. If I can provide you a product or service that enhances your life, or take an existing product and make it better, faster, cheaper or easier, I am a capitalist. Capitalism is based on serving your fellow man. Capitalism is based on finding a need and filling it. Finding a problem and coming up with a solution. Finding a frustration and fixing it. Every advancement made in civilization has been because of capitalism. Every comfort you enjoy—from your TV, car, coffee, air conditioning, electric blanket and a million other things—are because someone found a need and filled it, and often became wealthy in the process.

Capitalism also provides jobs for millions of people, as well as health insurance. Capitalists are not "greedy rich people." The opposite is true: Most of what they make goes back to employees in salary, health care, and buying materials from other businessmen and women. Everyone wins in capitalism.

Capitalism is based on voluntary cooperation. You are not forced to do business with anyone, work for anyone, or buy or sell with anyone. You get to choose. So Capitalism is in reality the greatest force for good on the planet today. When done according to principle, it increases prosperity, ends poverty, improves your quality of life, and everyone wins.

What has this got to do with the IRS?

THE PRESIDENT, CONGRESS AND IRS KILLS CAPITALISM.

Like millions of small business owners in America, my wife and I are _sick_ of the IRS. It takes us an average of *500 hours a year* just to keep up with the IRS paperwork. It *costs us tens of thousands of dollars* just to prepare the tax forms every year. Every week we get another letter from someone in the IRS office who has no idea what they are doing, telling us we owe them X amount of dollars. Then we have to spend hours gathering the paperwork to show them we don't owe anything. The IRS sends a letter saying we were right, and a week later we get the same letter telling us we owe them and we have to go through the whole process over again.

How does this affect you? I have to pass on those IRS costs to you, so you pay more. I have to waste time on the IRS so my customer service quality goes down. I finally get so frustrated that I shut down the business. Who wants to stay in business when the IRS takes over 30% of what I make, and then gives me grief all year long? It is not worth it. So you just lost your job, you no longer have health insurance, my suppliers lose my business so they soon go under, and everyone suffers.

Imagine if all this were done away. No more dealing with the IRS. No more forms to fill out. No more paperwork. No more April 15 deadlines. No more wasted time. No more trying to figure out what you can deduct. Every American equal. Imagine having all that extra time to work your business, spend time with your family, or relax. Think of all the tens of thousands of dollars you will save every year that you can invest, take a vacation, or give to your favorite charity. Think of the stress you will no longer have to deal with. Just think how all America would prosper.

Let's do it. Sign the petition at www.close theirsnow.com. Pass this book out to everyone you know, encourage everyone you know to purchase the book! Make a $10.00 investment with HEIRS so we can continue to get the word out and win the battle in Congress.

CHAPTER 12
SUMMARY

IT IS BEYOND HUMAN COMPREHENSION HOW
U.S. PRESIDENTS, CONGRESS, U.S. TREASURY
AND THE IRS HAVE ADDED TO THE COMPLEX-
ITY OF OUR MODERN DAY TAX SYSTEM SINCE
PRESIDENT LINCOLN SIGNED IT INTO LAW ON
JULY 1, 1862.

Is there any wonder why *no one in America* knows
and understands our current tax system after 150
years? It is broken beyond repair, and is unsustainable.

It makes you wonder what the 545 politicians in
Washington are thinking when they continue to com-
plicate a 150-year-old tax system instead of replacing
it. Then they wonder why their approval rating is down
to 9%? My 10-year-old daughter could do a better job
of running the White House and Congress.

WHAT IS THE SOLUTION?

THE PRESIDENT AND CONGRESS SHOULD
VOTE TO ELIMINATE OUR TOTAL TAX SYSTEM
NOW. THIS IS NOT UNUSUAL; PAST PRESI-
DENTS AND CONGRESS CLOSED THE IRS
THREE TIMES BEFORE. THE SUPREME
COURT ALSO DECLARED IT UNCONSTITU-
TIONAL AND CLOSED IT ONCE.

Throw out our current tax system and close down
the IRS now and replace it with a simple:
10% NATIONAL SALES TAX.
EVERYONE PAYS ON RETAIL PURCHASES
EXCEPT

**EDUCATION AND MEDICAL. IT IS SO SIM-
PLE IT CAN BE
EXPLAINED IN FOUR WORDS.
YOU BUY, YOU PAY**

No other tax system out there is as simple and less expensive as the ten percent National Sales Tax.

WHAT WOULD IT ACCOMPLISH?

1. A projected two million jobs would be added per year, many of them high-paying jobs.
2. Business and corporate tax would be eliminated.
3. American businesses would immediately have up to a 35% competitive advantage.
4. Without business income tax, the 30,000 current U.S. companies overseas would start moving back immediately.
5. Almost another one thousand businesses per year would stop moving out of America.
6. The two trillion dollars U.S. companies have overseas would now start coming home.
7. The U.S. is the ONLY Westernized country that still has an income tax on our businesses. For the first time our businesses would have a level playing field.
8. Due to our income tax laws, wealthy Americans and other have close to $12 Trillion dollars overseas. By eliminating our current tax system, this money would start coming home fast.
9. All the above would put Americans back to work and increase our standard of living.

Remember the honest taxpayers pay between fifty-two percent and fifty-seven percent of their income for taxes. America wants a simple, fair, level tax field where everyone pays his or her fair share.

> "A politician is someone who feels a great debt to his fellow man....which debt he proposes to pay off with your money."
> G. Gordon Liddy

> "The desire of any worker to keep what she has already earned through her labors is not greed. However the desire to grab more of other people's money does indeed qualify as greed...government greed."
> R. Lloyd Billingsley,
> Pacific Research Institute

CHAPTER 13

WHAT YOU CAN DO NOW TO HELP CLOSE DOWN THE IRS

TAKE ACTION!

Sign up online at: *www.closetheirsnow.com.*

We need only your name and email, and we promise not to add you to any other mail list. We respect your privacy. Once we have your information we can keep you updated on progress, rallies, and news.

Vote online. To abolish the IRS and go to a simple 10% National Sales Tax, simply go to the same site, *www.closetheirsnow.com* and add your information and check the box. *We need millions of votes.* With these votes we can force the Congress to act. As the votes pour in we will send them weekly to your Congressmen and to the White house. Every week the politicians in Washington will get bombarded with thousands of new votes. Your voice cannot be ignored.

Spread the word. Please send the links on the website to everyone on your email, Facebook, Twitter and any other method you can. Urge EVERYONE YOU KNOW to join our ranks.

Buy the book, - buy as many as you can and pass them out. We need millions of books to flood across the nation. Only $5.00 plus shipping, and in mass quantities you can get them much cheaper. See our online store.

Buy the E-book. Once you do, ask everyone you know to do the same. Spread it virally in every way you can.

Become a member of **HEIRS.**

Help

Eliminate

I

R

S

It is going to take money to do this. We are running this very efficiently, from home offices, with little over-head. The money is needed for web expense, for organizing rallies, correspondence, and most of all the expense it will take to get this through Congress.

WE ARE SPECIFICALLY ASKING FOR EVERY AMERICAN TO INVEST $10.00 WITH US.

If ONE OUT OF 10 Americans invested just $10.00, we would have the power to shut the IRS down overnight. Think about that. The average American makes $42,000 a year, but gives $14,000 back in taxes. Just invest $10.00 with us that you would nor-mally give to Uncle Sam and think how much you will save over the next few years with the IRS abolished. We can't do this without money. So, we encourage you to make a $10.00 contribution. You can do this online at: www.closetheirsnow.com.

When we do a rally, come and join us. We will notify you of all rallies by email in your state. When we ask you to forward an email to a national political leader, take one minute to do it. We have a specific plan in place to do hundreds of talk shows, TV and radio interviews, and get massive press to bring this to the masses.

Share your ideas. We invite your input. This is your movement. We learn from you. Email us in short, concise, and simple language your thoughts and ideas at: info@closetheirsnow.com.

Understand this movement spans all political persuasions. We will not get involved in Republican, Democrat, Libertarian, left, right, Independent, or other political labels.

WE ARE ALL AMERICANS WHO ARE UNITED IN ONE GOAL: ABOLISH THE IRS AND GO TO A 10% NATIONAL SALES TAX.

CHAPTER 14
IS THERE ONE TRUE AMERICAN POLITICIAN LEFT?

We are launching this drive in March of 2012. It is an election year. If there is a presidential candidate who is a genuine American and wants to win, then run on this issue. I guarantee you a landslide victory.

Is there a true Congressman or Senator who has not sold their soul to the special interest groups? Is there one of you in Washington who has a pure heart and is willing to stand for, "We the people?" Do any of the 545 leaders of this great nation have the character and principle to be honest, and fiscally responsible? Do any of you have the integrity to stand up to the corruption that prevails on Capitol Hill and be a voice of reason and common sense? Is there one of you who will uphold the constitution and do what is right, not politically correct?

If there is such a one, contact me. I know we can get the majority of the nation behind you. We just need one leader. One great one. One man or woman of impeccable character, honesty, integrity, and guts. One role model we can be proud of. One person we can have faith in. One person who loves the USA and would give his or her life to protect it and keep it great.

If there is no such one in 2012, then I will be that person. By the mid term elections in 2014, we will have millions of fellow Americans rallied to this revolution. I will lead you and not stop till we have accomplished our mission. With the same iron will, grit and tenacity it took to walk across America in 100 days, I will work for you and not rest till we have abolished the IRS, voted the 10% National Sales Tax, and brought sanity and fiscal responsibility back to Capital Hill.

Let's roll up our sleeves and go to work,

Leo Schreven Chairman
HEIRS Inc.

APPENDIX

Dr. Steven Chu
Secretary of Energy
1000 Independence Avenue SW
Washington D.C. 20585

Dear Dr. Chu:

Create one million new jobs per year for five years.

How? You and your colleagues can make this one of the top priorities to save America since becoming energy sufficient is the number one national security concern. This can be solved by producing all our energy needs right here in America.

This can be accomplished at zero cost.

How? Very simple. We import 17 million barrels of oil per day, much from our enemies or quasi enemies, except Canada and Mexico, at a cost of $350 to 700 billion dollars, depending on the price of crude oil, per year, plus we are fighting two wars primarily to protect our foreign oil supply. Between the imports and wars, we are spending way over one TRILLION dollars per year needlessly, especially Iraq and Afghanistan don't even want us in their countries.

What we need desperately is for you and the rest of the U.S. leaders to harness the country 24/7/365 like we did in World War II so support our 16,500,000 troops and win the horrible world war, which we did because every American was **FOCUSED ON ONE THING** – winning the war. I know I was there and did my bountiful share proudly.

I am suggesting the government take the lead to be the gigantic catalyst to mobilize the country into action ninety miles per hour. Please refer to the enclosed flow chart for one way it could happen.

Alternative fuels.

We have at least eight alternative fuels with **NO RAW MATERIAL COST**. Why not expand this first and then fuels with raw material cost. Please refer to the enclosed list.

In summary, in five years we could be fifty percent energy self-sufficient and in eight years 100 percent. This is realistic and doable.

Advantages

1. Increase national security.
2. Create one million new jobs annually minimum for at least five years at no cost. As we produce more energy at home we would send less overseas until it becomes zero.
3. Break Opec's back.
4. Break Russia's new initiated natural gas cartel.
5. Keep fuel cost low for America and world.
6. Sell new technology overseas.
7. We would stop the flow of dollars overseas from 350 billion dollars minimum to over one trillion annually.
8. A highly profitable way to use a portion of the stimulus package for some energy infrastructure.
9. Reduce cost of food by eliminating wheat and corn – our number one on two
   foods, for fuel.
10. Plus dozens of others.

Sincerely, A great admirer of yours,

Paul S. Damazo, Author

Retired Chairman / CEO of

Versitron Industries
40 – Year Registered Industrial Engineer
PSD/nb
Enclosure

NO RAW MATERIAL COST ALTERNATIVE FUELS

1. **Hydroelectric:** <u>The oldest and by far the most widely used alternative energy.</u> It is the most abundant renewable energy. <u>71.5 percent of all renewable energy come from hydropower</u> today. Of the 80,000 U.S. dams, only 2,400 have hydro plants, which could add one to four more generators per plant fairly rapidly. The we need to install generators to dams that have none. Plus build more dams with maximum generations of electricity. Remember it is domestic, it is affordable and it is reliable 24/7/365, not like wind and solar. **Expand rapidly. Don't even think of destroying some existing dams out west.**

2. **Geothermal Energy:** This energy has been in use since 1820, at least. Today geothermal energy costs four to seven cents/K.W.H. close to cost of wind power and a lot cheaper than solar. **"There is 50,000 times more heat energy contained in the first six miles of the earth's crust <u>than in all the plant's oil and natural gas resources combined</u>, according to the Earth Policy Institute. Expand rapidly.**

3. **Ocean Water Power: The earth is covered with 70 percent water.** The world energy council, a global research group, estimates **<u>ocean waterpower equates to more than</u>**

5,000 times the current global electrical demand. Thank God we finally have 100 or so research and producing ocean water power projects. We need to expand rapidly and gigantically.

4. **Offshore Wind Farms:** Out of sight ocean wind farms are much more reliable due to the steady stronger winds and more reliable than land based wind or solar.

5. **Biofuels from grass and other no cost waste products.**

6. **Land Wind:** Again no cost for raw materials.

7. **Solar:** Another no cost raw material.

8. **Air – Powered Cars:** Years old with off the shelf technology producing zero pollution motors and cars can be sold under $20,000.

SOME FUELS WITH RAW MATERIAL COST

9. **Natural Gas:** Starting in six months all trucks of every size and many cars should be built to consume compressed natural gas. It is forty percent cheaper and it is one of the cleanest, safest and most useful of all energy sources. Install the national gas line from Alaska now and create many jobs rapidly.

10. **Hydrogen Fuel Cells:** One very big cost is energy fro the process. Solution: Build small <u>mini</u> safe nuclear power plants adjacent to large hydrogen fuel cell power generation. Mini nuclear power plants can produce electricity for .02/K.W.

11. **Large Nuclear Power Plants:** Today France produces eighty percent of its electricity from nuclear power only. Many nuclear power plants are being built world wide except in the

U.S. with very few on the drawing board. One of the quickest, easiest way to solve our electricity needs at a very low cost per K.W.H.

12. **Clean Coal:** The technology is in existence in the U.S. to convert coal into a clear liquid fuel for transportation, that is entirely free from sulfur and other impurities that cause air pollution all for $35 per barrel. Why not expand now at 1000 miles per hour? The U.S. has a 300 year supply of coal. Also use clean coal as an energy source.

13. **Hydride Batteries:** and other batteries for autos, rather than purchasing overseas.

14. **Sugar Cane:** Use high grade sugar content like Brazil uses to produce ethanol instead of wheat and corn. Using food for fuel is a total disaster.

15. **Drill, drill, drill for oil. Now on land and sea, including Alaska:** We need to do this to keep our 350-700 billion dollars we use to purchase oil at home. **This is for the short term while we develop all of the above.**

Hawaii could be 100 percent fuel self sufficient and not have to import a drop of oil in four years if the state would go back to growing sugar cane for ethanol using the new hybrid cane seed from Brazil. Hawaii has the highest gas prices in the U.S.

Summary: It is time to use our own resources to become energy independent. We have more than we could ever use right in our own backyard.

Compiled by: Paul S. Damazo, 6134 Clarendon Court, Riverside, California 92506 (951)787-7136

DISCLAIMER

This book is designed to inspire you into action and to provide accurate and authentic information in regard to the subject matter covered. Factual material has been obtained from sources believed to be reliable, but is not guaranteed. All examples are for illustrative purposes only and are not to be construed as recommendations, advice, or tax counsel. The authors and publisher are not engaged in rendering legal, accounting, or other professional service. If legal or other expert assistance is required, the authors and publisher strongly recommend that the reader should contact his or her own professional advisors.

This publication is protected under the US Copyright Act of 1976 and all other applicable international, federal, state and local laws, and all rights are reserved, including resale rights:

YOU *ARE ALLOWED* TO FREELY DISTRIBUTE INFORMATION ABOUT THE E-BOOK TO ANYONE IN THE WORLD THROUGH:

E-mail

Electronic bulletin board

Web sites

FTP site,

Newsgroups

Or any social Media like Facebook, Twitter, etc.

WE WANT THIS BOOK TO GO VIRAL AS FAST AS POSSIBLE! SO HELP US GET THE INFORMATION OUT.

WE ASK ONLY TWO FAVORS:

Encourage everyone you contact to go online to www.closetheirsnow.com and vote.

Encourage everyone to make the $10.00 investment online so we can have the necessary funds to get this through Congress. (For a $5.00 investment an e-book is sent free)

Please note that much of this publication is based on personal experience and anecdotal evidence. Although the authors and publisher have made every reasonable attempt to achieve complete accuracy of the content in this publication, they assume no responsibility for errors or omissions. Also, you should use this information as you see fit, and at your own risk. Your particular situation may not be exactly suited to the examples illustrated here; in fact, it's likely that they won't be the same, and you should adjust your use of the information and recommendations accordingly.

Limit of Liability and Disclaimer of Warranty: The publisher has used its best efforts in preparing this book, and the information provided herein is provided "as is." HEIRS Inc. makes no representation or warranties with respect to the accuracy or completeness of the contents of this book and specifically disclaims any implied warranties of merchantability or fitness for any particular purpose and shall in no event be liable for any loss of profit or any other commercial damage, including but not limited to special, incidental, consequential, or other damages.

Trademarks: This book identifies product names and services known to be trademarks, registered trademarks, or service marks of their respective holders. They are used throughout this book in an editorial fashion only. In addition, terms suspected of being trademarks, registered trademarks, or service marks have been appropriately capitalized, HEIRS Inc. cannot attest to the accuracy of this information. Use of a term in this book should not be regarded as affecting the validity of any trademark, registered trademark, or service mark.

NOTHING IN THIS PUBLICATION IS TO BE TAKEN AS ANTI-GOVERNMENT OR POLITICAL SLANDER. HEIRS INC. IS LEADING A PEACEFUL, LEGAL, ETHICAL, AND SOLUTION BASED MOVEMENT TO CLOSE THE IRS IN FAVOR OF A 10% NATIONAL SALES TAX ALTERNATIVE. FELLOW AMERICANS WHO VOTE THEIR CONSCIENCE ARE ENCOURAGED TO MAINTAIN THE HIGHEST STANDARDS OF EXCELLENT CHARACTER, AND TO CONDUCT THEMSELVES WITH THE HIGHEST STANDARDS AS GENUINE AMERICAN, LAW ABIDING, LAW ENFORCEMENT RESPECTING, ORDERLY, AND RESPECTFUL CITIZENS WHO SEEK TO BUILD THE GREATEST COUNTRY ON EARTH, THE UNITED STATES OF AMERICA.